D1622438

Hey, God?
Yes, Charles.

Hey, God?
Yes, Charles.

*CONVERSATIONS ON
LIFE, LOSS, AND LOVE*

REBECCA H. COOPER

TURNER
PUBLISHING COMPANY

Turner Publishing Company
424 Church Street • Suite 2240 • Nashville, Tennessee 37219
445 Park Avenue • 9th Floor • New York, New York 10022

www.turnerpublishing.com

Hey, God? Yes, Charles.

Cover and book design: Maddie Cothren

Library of Congress Cataloging-in-Publication Data

Cooper, Rebecca H. (Rebecca Haynes)
Hey God, Yes Charles / by Rebecca H. Cooper.
pages cm
ISBN 978-1-63026-886-2 (pbk.)
1. Grief--Religious aspects--Christianity. 2. Cooper, Charles Marvin, Jr., 1949-2007. I. Title.
BV4908.C65 2015   248.8'66092--dc23   2015009481

Printed in the United States of America
15 16 17 18 19 20 0 9 8 7 6 5 4 3 2

To my parents.

OBITUARY

CHARLES MARVIN COOPER, JR, age 58, of Brentwood, Tennessee, died November 26, 2007 from complications following emergency open-heart surgery in Atlanta, Georgia. Born in Cannon County, TN, on November 12, 1949, he was a graduate of the University of Tennessee. At the time of his death, he was Chief Information Officer for Alliance Surgery, Inc. He was an active member of Johnson's Chapel United Methodist Church and recent Board chair for the nonprofit organization closest to his heart, Progress, Inc. Preceded in death by his parents, Charles and Evelyn Cooper, he is survived by his wife of 38 years, Rebecca Haynes Cooper (Becky); brother, Bobby Cooper; daughters, Angela (Brandon) Tubbs and Rita (Jason) Dodd; beloved grandchildren, MaKayla, Madelyn, and Scarlett; Becky's parents R.T. and Diana Haynes of Shelbyville, Tennessee, to whom he was more son than son-in-law; aunts, Shirley Cooper and Ethleen Bazzell; and several cousins. Charles loved his family and friends, animals, music, travel, and (most of the time) Big Orange football. Memorial services will be held at 1:00 pm, Saturday, December 1, 2007, followed by a Celebration of Charles/Butch/Coop/Papa's life at Christ Church, Wallace Chapel, 15354 Old Hickory Blvd, Nashville (615) 834-6171. Memorial contributions may be made to Progress, Inc, (319 Ezell Pike, Nashville 37217) or Johnson's Chapel UMC (210 High Lea Rd, Brentwood 37027) or the charity of your choice.

PROLOGUE

SUNDAY, NOVEMBER 11, 2007, I watched my husband drive out of sight, heading from our Nashville condo to his office and apartment in Atlanta. I never saw him conscious again.

MONDAY, NOVEMBER 12, was his fifty-eighth birthday. Since he would be out of town, our granddaughters and I had made him a cake and celebrated before he left on that Sunday.

WEDNESDAY, NOVEMBER 14, Charles caught me at my desk, calling just to let me know that he'd had some pretty weird pain radiating down his back. It subsided, and he was sure it was nothing, but the company nurse who just happened to be in the office that day heard what happened and insisted on calling 911 as a precaution. He assured me he was already feeling better—heck, he was in perfect health, it was probably gas! —and he'd call again once they gave him the okay at the ER. We swapped love yous. I didn't even get out of my chair.

MONDAY, NOVEMBER 26, at 2:40 a.m., despite hundreds, maybe thousands, of prayers, my precious husband died. The initial diagnosis was thoracic aortic dissection—the exact same thing that happened to John Ritter. Emergency open-heart surgery was followed by complications including acute respiratory distress syndrome, pneumonia, and various lung infections. We had been married almost thirty-nine years.

In the following year, I learned that the connection with someone you love doesn't cease with death. Charles was always bigger than life, and his presence—his love, his humor, these conversations—was just as real after his death.

For better, for worse, I started scribbling down what I was overhearing in heaven.

I was done talking to God. Charles, as it turned out, was not.

ABOUT FIVE MONTHS
AFTER CHARLES DIED

I'm spending the night at my dad's house, though I know I won't sleep well. I will dream about Charles.

I will lean over the terrace rail and see him walking toward me down the sidewalk. He opens the gate and we embrace.

"Where have you been?" I ask.

"You know I've been in heaven," he replies. "Where have you been?"

"Oh honey," I say, "you know I've been in hell."

"Hey, God?"

"Yes, Charles."

"Becky feels guilty about letting me die."

"Becky let you die?" God frowned. "She spent thirteen days vetting the hospital and the doctors, getting second opinions, researching the internet nonstop, and calling in every medical connection she had. Gal in the ICU asked her if she was a nurse for Pete's sake."

Charles was solemn. "Yeah, but we always—*always*—had each other's backs. That last hour by my side, watching my numbers drop, she thought she had failed me."

"Your oxygen," God whispered, "is what failed you."

"Hey, God?"

"Yes, Charles."

"Bettye brought Becky a journal today and encouraged her to write, write, write."

God nodded. "I noticed that's what Bettye did when Chester died fifteen years ago. Is Becky doing it?"

"She is, but I don't know. Her first entry says she's so angry and sad that she can't stand it."

"She will stand it," God predicted.

"Hey, God?"

"Yes, Charles."

"Today, Becky was telling Armstrong about the strangest reality: how much there is to do after someone dies. Literally one minute she's standing by my bed and the only thing in the world she has to do is watch me breathe, and in the next minute, I'm dead and the hospital is asking who will pick me up."

"To which, of course, she has no answer," God replied.

"Hey, God?"

"Yes, Charles."

"Did you hear Scott speaking at my celebration of life gathering after my service? One time on a business trip he saw me zipping to the bathroom in the middle of the night and discovered I'm a commando sleeper. He told everyone that!!"

God winked. "What a great start to that rock-n-roll funeral you always said you wanted!"

"Hey, God?"

"Yes, Charles."

"Becky snagged my T-shirt off the back of the bathroom door in Atlanta. She's taking it to bed with her at night."

God was practical. "Nothing wrong with the comfort of cotton."

"Hey, God?"

"Yes, Charles."

"Today Becky was reading cards she saved that I've written her over the years. She was reminding me that I said I would always be beside her."

"Well, Charles, you are."

"Hey, God?"

"Yes, Charles."

"Sports question."

"Shoot."

"You know, December 1, the day of my service, Becky had the memorial first, then a celebration of life with stories, videos, food, laughter, and tears."

"Sure, rock-n-roll, I was there."

"Well," Charles continued, "remember, God, the Tennessee Vols played the SEC championship that day and she even had a television in there, and we *lost*. I don't mean to be critical, but couldn't you have, you know, just that one time . . . ?"

"Charles, Charles, Charles," God admonished. "No I could not!"

"Hey, God?"

"Yes, Charles."

"You love me, right?"

God smiled. "You're *here* aren't you?!"

"Hey, God?"

"Yes, Charles."

"If I was going to die anyway, why did we waste thirteen days and almost $300,000?"

"Oh," God reflected, "they weren't wasted."

"Mmmm," Charles replied. "Blue Cross might disagree."

"Hey, God?"

"Yes, Charles."

"One of the insurance companies called Becky. They have to meet with her."

"Why?" God was puzzled.

"Because my newest policy is less than two years old. They requested this meeting to review my medical records to be sure everything was revealed on the original application. Becky's thinking, *Knock yourself out, and if you find anything new, I'd like to hear it.*"

"I know," said God. "She would like to knock somebody out if they missed something."

"I think she'd just like to knock somebody out, period."

"Hey, God?"

"Yes, Charles."

"Becky was trying to get the cable turned off at our apartment in Atlanta the day the Armstrongs came with their truck."

"Yeah?"

"The lady on the phone kept asking what the problem was and Becky kept trying to avoid the real answer. She told her, no, there were no service issues, and we're not changing companies, yes, we're moving, and no, we don't need service elsewhere. Finally, Becky had to say, 'My husband died.'"

"That," said God, "will stop the interrogation."

"Hey, God?"

"Yes, Charles."

"Becky met with our attorneys today. They're getting the petition ready to go to court next week."

"How is Becky handling that?" God asked.

"Today, I think, just felt surreal."

"I can understand that."

"Hey, God?"

"Yes, Charles."

"Becky went to Target today to buy an iPod for our bedroom."

"That's good."

"Maybe. We had planned to get one for Christmas, but all she wants to listen to now are all the songs that make her sad."

"Uh oh."

"But the funny part is she knows she has no clue how to make the thing work. I was our technical guru. I saw her look up toward me as she left the cashier."

God was curious. "Did she see anything helpful?"

Charles shook his head. "Just Target's ceiling tiles."

"God?"

"Yes, Charles."

"Becky wants her husband back."

"I know, son."

"Hey, God?"

"Yes, Charles."

"Becky had dinner tonight with our friends Roger and Gloria. They have to go back to Guatemala tomorrow."

"Good people," God approved.

"So many folks talk about my death being Your will. Drives Becky crazy. Roger and Gloria don't buy it either."

God was pleased. "Smart too."

"Hey, God?"

"Yes, Charles."

"I'm worried about Becky."

"Anything specific?" God asked.

"She's running on adrenaline, not eating, crying. She needs me."

"She," God proclaimed, "has Me."

"Hey, God?"

"Yes, Charles."

"You know that speaker and iPod Becky bought the other day?"

"I do."

"Well she got the speaker hooked up and tonight she figured out how to load the little battery in the remote."

"She figure out the iPod yet?" asked God.

"Nah," said Charles, "she's still looking at the box."

"No need to rush into anything," confirmed God.

"Hey, God?"

"Yes, Charles."

"Did you know Becky sent thank-you notes to my doctors at St. Joseph's?"

God grinned. "She does know that you died, right?"

Charles had to belly laugh. "Very funny. We both thought they tried, tried, tried to save me. And, you know—"

God finished the thought. "She's from the South."

"Hey, God?"

"Yes, Charles."

"Becky wants to put a bullet into an oxygen monitor."

The puzzled look on God's face was priceless. "Huh?"

"She hated watching that monitor the last day of my life. She wants to shoot one."

"Hey, God?"

"Yes, Charles."

"My first *Sports Illustrated* came today. Becky's been reading it."

"Okay . . . "

"The subscription was my last birthday present from her and her parents. It came after I died. Becky has been remembering when she gave it to me and how she told me it was gonna be the nonswimsuit version. About two weeks later, I looked over at her and casually asked, 'There's really no such thing as two Sports Illustrated versions, right?'"

"You two are a mess!" God smiled.

"Hey, God?"

"Yes, Charles."

"Becky's listening to Dolly and Vince sing 'I Will Always Love You.'"

"Oh, dear."

"It reminds her of that moment in the ICU when she saw that one tear slide down my cheek."

"Hey, God?"

"Yes, Charles."

"Even though I was never conscious, every time she was allowed into the ICU, Becky told me what was going on, exactly who had called or e-mailed, and who was visiting. I wish I could let everyone know how much I appreciate all that."

"Well," said God, "a thank you note might scare some folks!"

Charles smiled. "I'll trust Becky to handle it."

God nodded. "Good plan."

"Hey, God?"

"Yes, Charles."

"Tracy just left. She made Becky a Charles Cooper photo album."

"Nice."

"Memories of me and thoughts she wrote within three days of my death."

"I saw that. You sound like a pretty good guy."

Charles grinned. "Well, you know Tracy's an excellent judge of character."

"Get out of here, Charles!"

"Hey, God?"

"Yes, Charles."

"Becky had dinner with Nan tonight. Thank God, she doesn't think my death was Your will." Charles eyes twinkled.

"Another one for our side," said God.

"Hey, God?"

"Yes, Charles."

"Becky's Sunday School lesson today was about prayer."

"Uh oh."

"Yeah, that was a tough class for her. So much praying and I died anyway."

"It's not easy for me either, Charles."

"Hey, God?"

"Yes, Charles."

"Keith and Pam spent hours today showing Becky how iTunes works with the iPod. Keith said, 'Charles could have done all this in half the time but somewhere in there he'd have lost his glasses!'"

God laughed. "Yes, you would have and probably an umbrella too!"

"Hey, God?"

"Yes, Charles."

"Pam and Keith just called Becky to see if she would go out to eat with them. She made an excuse."

"She should have gone."

"Well, the mail just came. My first life insurance check was in there. Whew. She felt like she could fake being okay over the phone but not in person."

"Probably better for Pam and Keith," acknowledged God.

"Oh dear, God?"

"What, son."

"You know our little granddaughter Maddie. She's five. She was standing next to the stereo—"

"Listening to 'Mary Did You Know?'" God said gently, "your favorite Christmas hymn that was sung so beautifully at your service."

"That was Ellie and Jackie." Charles smile was sober. "But Maddie was listening to the song, looked at my picture, and said, 'I can't get pneumonia out of my head.'"

"Whew," said God.

"God?"

"Yes, Charles."

"Becky's mama just got here!"

"Yes, I saw her coming."

"Christmas Eve, God—four weeks after me. That sure is hard on everybody. But gosh, I love Grandma."

God smiled. "Don't we all."

"Hey, God?"

"Yes, Charles."

"It's Christmas Day. In Becky's journal she wrote, 'Mama died last night. I can't write anything today except I need you.'"

"I'm so sorry, Charles."

"God?"

"Right here, Charles."

"Becky went out to buy shoes for Maddie and MaKayla to wear to her mother's funeral. She was disappointed by the crowd."

"Packed?" God asked.

"No," explained Charles, "just the opposite. Pretty sparse, which aggravated Becky. She was hoping for mayhem so she could smack somebody."

"Maybe Afghanistan," offered God.

"Hey, God?"

"Yes, Charles."

"Becky read the Verizon bill last night. By following the calls, she can chronicle almost every step from my first call to her on November 14 until I died on November 26. The call that really got to her was the last one right before they took me into the operating room. How could she have known?"

God wanted to prepare Charles. "There will be a lot more ways for her to relive the pain and surprise of your death, son."

"Hey, God?"

"Yes, Charles."

"I was telling you Becky was reading the Verizon bill last night. Did I tell you it was almost $600?"

God winced. "Well, that'll bring tears to your eyes."

"Hey, God?"

"Yes, Charles."

"Barb spent a lot of time on the phone with Becky yesterday. She thinks she may be experiencing depression and really does need to find someone to talk to."

"What was Becky's response?"

"Well, she didn't exactly disagree—but after that conversation she talked to BJ."

"Who said . . . ?"

"Basically, talk to Mr. Zoloft."

"Hey, God?"

"Yes, Charles."

"Barb called Becky Saturday and they talked again for a long time."

"Did it help?"

"Well, in her doctor voice, she got Becky to agree to try to find a therapist."

"Couldn't hurt."

"Hey, God?"

"Yes, Charles."

"It's January. Becky's visiting her daddy. They're sitting around the kitchen table talking, reminiscing."

"Well, Charles, they need to do that," God reassured.

"Oh, I know," Charles agreed. "But R.T. can sure hit the nail on the head. He shared a great memory—decades old—looked at Becky, and said, 'Why is it in those days you don't think about these days?'"

"Hey, God?"

"Yes, Charles."

"Becky got under our bathroom sink today and organized all the crap. Oh, can I say *crap*?"

God didn't care. "Go ahead."

"Anyway all my stuff she brought home from under our sink in Atlanta and tossed in the cabinet."

"Small task, but tough."

"It was at moments. Then she'd go back and look at what she'd done and take comfort in the organization."

"She is an organizer," God acknowledged.

"Hey, God?"

"Yes, Charles."

"Becky finally made an appointment with that shrink who was recommended."

"That's probably good, Charles."

"I hope so. She's not so sure."

"She misses you, Charles. Even I realize nothing can change that."

Hey, God? Yes, Charles.

"You know what, God?"

"What, Charles?"

"I died six weeks ago and people are still calling and checking on Becky. I appreciate that."

God looked down with satisfaction. "Me too."

"Hey, God?"

"Yes, Charles."

"Becky needs to call Tony and get her roots done, but that feels disrespectful to her. She and I always went together."

"Well," said God, "that's because you two could turn a haircut into an adventure. But she won't let those roots grow out much longer, and that'll be good."

"Hey, God?"

"Yes, Charles."

"My brother, Bobby, had to be hospitalized today, which is especially scary for a mentally challenged person. Becky is beside herself."

"But," God pointed out, "he gets great care from a great organization."

"No kidding. Progress has been, well, a Godsend."

"You're welcome."

"And Becky has already started the process of becoming his conservator since my death."

"Well, Charles, you knew she'd do that."

"Yeah, but I always handled his care and this scares her to death."

"Hey, God?"

"Yes, Charles."

"Becky finally got Tony to finish her hair today. She's going to church with her daddy again tomorrow."

"Well," said God, "that's good, right?"

"Yeah, but you know those photo cards Becky sent out as thank you notes?" Charles continued, "Tony told her he has that picture of me back on his work shelf and his wife told him her picture better be there too!"

God chuckled. "If it wasn't, I bet it's there now!"

"Hey, God?"

"Yes, Charles."

Charles was enthused. "You're gonna love this. Our neighbor, Ali, brought Becky a jar she made. It's full of spiritual vitamins. Each day Becky pulls out a piece of paper, and there's a special Bible verse, all about love."

God smiled. "You are absolutely right. I do *love* that!"

"Hey, God?"

"Yes, Charles."

"Becky doesn't want to wash the sheets."

"What do you mean?" asked God.

"Remember I told you about the last weekend before my birthday when I was home with her and our granddaughters in Nashville?" reminded Charles.

"Go on," said God.

"Well, that was the last time we slept on those sheets together, and she doesn't want to change them."

God was realistic. "Gotta wash the sheets."

Hey, God? Yes, Charles.

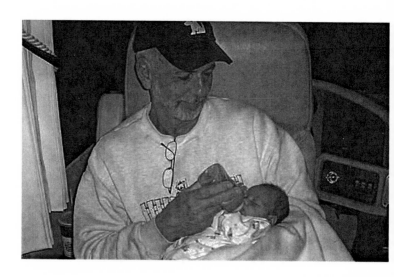

"Hey, God?"

"Yes, Charles."

"Becky saw that shrink this week."

"Helpful?" asked God.

"Well, she wants to be sure she knows everything she needs to know. She wants somebody, anybody, to tell her the rules."

"There aren't any rules." God acknowledged.

Charles nodded. "That's what the doc said."

"Hey, God?"

"Yes, Charles."

"Becky got a letter from Bill. He wrote about a great conversation he and I once had about my theory of progressive revelation."

"Really?" God was interested but noncommittal.

"Yep." Charles was eager. "And I just thought I'd check. That's right isn't it?"

God grinned. "Tell you later."

"Hey, God?"

"Yes, Charles."

"Tonight Becky wanted to move the iPod stereo to the chest where the bedroom television is, but she had to figure out how to get it all plugged in. She was afraid if she unplugged the TV or the cable box she'd have to call the cable company all over again. When it all worked she was amazed and pleased with herself. *Then* she programmed the radio remote."

"Is that an accomplishment?" asked God.

"You have no idea. If I was there she wouldn't even try."

"But," said God, "you're not. So good for her."

"Hey, God?" Charles was laughing.

"Yes, Charles."

"Becky was able to move Rascal Flatts' 'Winner at a Losing Game' to her iPod tonight."

"Wow," said God. "That's great. But why is that funny?"

"She doesn't have a clue how she did it."

"Hey, God?"

"Yes, Charles."

"Scott called Becky today just to check on her. Adam called Saturday to see about dinner with him and Valerie. She got a card in the mail today from Bettye. The cousins call often. Ang calls from Utah. You know it's been over two months now, and of course the calls and messages are going to slack off."

"But," said God, "the support is still there. Your family and friends are—"

"Unbelievable," finished Charles.

"Hey, God?" Charles had to shout over the barking.

"Yes, Charles."

"We used to worry that when we got to Heaven our animals wouldn't be here."

God smiled, looking at the wagging dogs and swishing cats. "Oh, puhleeze."

February 12, 2008

"Hey, God?"

"Yes, Charles."

"Today's my mama's birthday."

"I know. Both your folks have been here a long time. Seen them yet?"

"Oh yeah." Charles was smiling.

"Hey, God?"

"Yes, Charles."

"I was in Becky's dream last night. She touched my skin. It was warm. How do we do that?"

"Oh," said God, "that's easy for us. The hard part is when she wakes up."

"Oh dear, God?"

"Yes, Charles."

"Did you hear Maddie say, 'I think if we start crying, God will start crying and give Papa back to us.'?"

"I heard it, Charles."

"Hey, God?" Charles was solemn.

"Yes, Charles."

"Becky's getting ready to go to court this morning to probate my will."

"Hard day," acknowledged God.

"She's been playing that new Eagles song, 'It's Your World Now.'"

"Lots of wisdom in those words," nodded God.

"Well, wisdom makes her cry."

"Hey, God?"

"Yes, Charles."

"Becky is still crying every day."

"That's normal, I think."

"Yeah, but it's going on three months now. I think she thought maybe it wouldn't be every day by now."

"There's no timetable, Charles," God confided.

"Hey, God?"

"Yes, Charles."

"Becky worked out with Shannon, her trainer, today—first time since I died."

"How was it?"

"Becky told her she was going for the sympathy routine."

God laughed. "Worth a shot."

"Hey, God?"

"Yes, Charles."

"Shannon worked out a deal with Becky to get everybody off her back for not eating."

"What's the deal?" God was curious.

"Three small meals and two snacks at least. You know she's a vegetarian. Think that's enough?"

"I think," God answered, "that's all she can do right now."

"Hey, God?"

"Yes, Charles."

"It's been almost three months. Becky's tried eating, not eating, drinking, not drinking, spending money, not spending money, reading, writing. This week she's been working on exercising. She just cries in the workout room. And she is so angry with you."

"Charles, you let *Me* worry about that."

"Hey, God?"

"Yes, Charles."

"The *Sports Illustrated* swimsuit edition came today. Becky held the cover up to my picture so I could see it."

God howled. "That is one good wife."

"Hey, God?"

"Yes, Charles."

"Becky just wished me a happy Valentine's Day."

"She loves you, Charles."

"Hey, God?"

"Yes, Charles."

"Becky got cards, messages, flowers, and even Barnes called her for Valentine's."

"I know," laughed God. "I heard her tell you she got more this year than from you last year."

Charles laughed too. "She's such a kidder."

"Hey, God?"

"Yes, Charles."

"Becky was walking Millie tonight, in the dark parking lot, crying. She just wants to see me again."

"Charles, I know."

"Hey, God?"

"Yes, Charles."

"Becky's need to touch me is physical. Sometimes she just reaches out her hands."

"I realize that Charles."

"*Can* we touch her?"

"We do, son. She just doesn't know it yet."

"God?"

"Yes, Charles."

"I've been dead eighty-six days. Shouldn't Becky feel better by now?"

"Charles, I don't think she wants to feel better."

February 23, 2008

"Hey, God?"

"Yes, Charles."

"Becky and Ri celebrated Granddaddy's eighty-fifth birthday today."

"Good for them," cheered God, "and him."

"Hey, God?"

"Yes, Charles."

"Today it's been exactly three months since I died. Becky's been struggling with that all day."

"Charles," God understood, "almost every day is going to be an anniversary of something."

"Hey, God?"

"Yes, Charles."

"Becky had to get the oil changed in the Pathfinder today. First time she's had to do that. Made her mad!"

"The oil made her mad?"

"The fact that I wasn't there to do it, that she had to pull in there and act like she knew which oil and how much."

"I see. Won't be the last time."

"Guy showed her the dipstick and all she could think was she felt like a dipstick."

"Hey, God?"

"Yes, Charles."

"Becky's looking at cars."

"Well, that's progress."

"She'll only look at something I already was talking about and that should be fine. But a funny thing happened tonight."

"Oh yeah?"

"She had talked to the salesman a couple of times. Tonight he asked if she was married, guess wanting to see if there was anybody else he had to sell. But she couldn't say it. She told him yes, she was married."

"Oops."

"Exactly. But later sitting in the car she told him the truth, burst into tears, and you know what happened?"

"He hit on her?"

"No! He asked if he could pray for her."

God couldn't stop smiling.

"Hey, God?"

"Yes, Charles."

"Becky bought that car today."

"That's good, right?"

"Well, the Pathfinder has well over 100,000 miles on it and she's driving up east to see Scarlett."

"That visit," said God, "will be good for both of them."

"Hey, God?"

"Yes, Charles."

"Becky picked up the new car today."

"Great."

"They were going over all the tech gadgets on it. As she was driving away, she looked up through the windshield and told me she knew how much I'd have loved all that stuff."

God was quick to point out, "We have some pretty cool stuff up here too."

"Hey, God?"

"Yes, Charles."

"Becky forgot to bathe today."

"What do you mean?"

"Well, she was getting ready to step out of the shower, and she looked up. Her washcloth was still dry, and she realized she'd forgotten to bathe."

"Charles, it takes your brain awhile to adjust to all this."

"But God, she's in the third month now."

"There is no timetable, son."

"Hey, God?"

"Yes, Charles."

"That was a great little snow for the first week of March."

"Wasn't it?"

"Rita was spending the night and she and Becky piled up on our bed. The view out to the courtyard was so pretty. Becky of course couldn't help but think about how I'd have enjoyed it."

"I believe you did, Charles."

"Hey, God?"

"Yes, Charles."

"Remember when we sold our house a couple of years ago in order to travel and then downsize?"

"I do."

"Becky just found out our old house will be back on the market. She drove by the other day. Her first reaction was she wanted it back."

"Oh, dear."

"Exactly. She ran that thought by her best friend BJ and Aunt Shirley, and they both told her the same thing."

"Which was?"

"That won't bring Charles back."

"Hey, God?"

"Yes, Charles."

"Becky thinks nobody will ever love her like I do."

"She's right." God was certain.

Charles turned away to hide the little, tiny grin.

Hey, God? Yes, Charles.

Hey, God? Yes, Charles.

"Hey, God?"

"Yes, Charles."

"Becky just paired her new Blackberry up to the new car."

"Wow." God was now aware of Becky's technical limitations.

"I know. Can I faint if I'm already dead?"

"Hey, God?"

"Yes, Charles."

"I'm so glad Becky and I took that year to travel and work from the road, but it's a wonder I didn't drive that bus off the side of a mountain."

"Not really," God stated.

"That would have taken us both out, which actually was always our plan to go together. Becky doesn't like me going alone."

"Don't expect she does."

"Hey, God?"

"Yes, Charles."

"Becky's getting ready to drive up to PA to see Scarlett. She just turned two."

"Wonderful."

"She's made her a photo book so she can see all her southern relatives but mostly so she'll know who I am."

"Equally wonderful."

"Hey, God?"

"Yes, Charles."

"Becky's packing the car tonight—she's leaving tomorrow to drive up to Pennsylvania and see Scarlett. You know we haven't seen her in months."

"You got a bad break in that timing, Charles, but I know Becky's glad to finally get the opportunity."

"Bittersweet though," Charles mused. "Always assumed we'd go up together."

"So go."

"Hey, God?"

"Yes, Charles."

"Becky just checked into Fairfield Inn, first night en route to PA."

"Good trip so far?"

"Yeah, bad weather finally moved out. But the first few minutes in that hotel room without me felt really funny."

"I know traveling without you is not something she wants to do."

Charles was beginning to see the picture. "One more thing to add to the sad list."

"It gets longer," God acknowledged, "before it gets shorter."

"Hey, God?"

"Yes, Charles."

"You know that year we traveled North America in our motor home, we laughed when we were done because we concluded we had somehow missed West Virginia."

"And your goal was to finish off all fifty states."

"Right. Well, she's taking the same route and debated zipping over to West Virginia to complete the list but I think she's decided to wait 'til she gets up here with me and maybe we can swoop down together."

God had to laugh. "Swoop?"

"Hey, God?"

"Yes, Charles."

"Becky was grinning up at me today—as she drove under the West Virginia sign!"

God beamed. "You didn't miss it!"

"Tickled her." Charles was tickled too.

"Hey, God?"

"Yes, Charles."

"Becky's got Scarlett this afternoon. Right off, that child noticed my ring that Becky wears."

"Of course"

"Becky told her, I love you and so does Papa. Scarlett responded with the perfect answer."

"Which was?"

"Yep."

"Hey, God?"

"Yes, Charles."

"Becky worries about her friends asking her to do stuff all the time. She so appreciates it, but sometimes she implies she's already booked just because she hates to subject them to her at a low moment. But you know she's pretty honest, and this kinda bothers her."

God was kind. "I won't count it against her."

"Hey, God?"

"Yes, Charles."

"Becky's having to complete some forms with a choice of *single* or *widowed*. Whew."

"Another moment of reality, Charles."

Charles was still. "She can hardly bring her pen to the paper."

what do I do with my heart

what do I do with my heart

what do I do with my heart

"Hey, God?"

"Yes, Charles."

"Becky's filling up a page writing that."

"She's been listening to that Eagles song again." God was matter-of-fact.

"Every day," said Charles.

"Hey, God?"

"Yes, Charles."

"Do you know Becky's hiding the new car from the neighbors?"

"She worried what they'll think about her?" God was curious.

"No," said Charles, "what they'll think about me."

"How so?"

"She doesn't want them to think she's being disrespectful to me."

"Hey, God?"

"Yes, Charles."

"Becky poured the orange juice on her blueberries this morning."

"I saw that."

"She feels so confused. Will that get better?"

"Oh, Charles," God explained, "her brain will adapt soon enough. It's her heart that will take awhile."

"Hey, God?"

"Yes, Charles."

"Why'd you set it up this way? This dying thing is so hard on everybody."

"Well, Charles . . ." God was funny-serious. "What would you suggest? Can't beam you up outta Starbucks."

"Hey, God?"

"Yes, Charles."

"Becky's got her list. She thinks if she can just not lose that list maybe she won't lose her mind either."

God hesitated. "That's a big responsibility for a piece of paper."

"Hey, God?"

"Yes, Charles."

"Everybody tells Becky that with time she will feel better."

"That's surely true."

"She thinks she'll just be able to fake it better."

"Hey, God?"

"Yes, Charles."

"You know Becky rarely drives the new car—she's been hiding it in the garage so our neighbors won't see it."

"I know."

"Well Friday she drove my old Pathfinder to her Daddy's to spend the night. Unfortunately she neglected to close the garage door when she left."

"So much for hiding the car."

"Hey, God?"

"Yes, Charles."

"Becky's been watching *Deal or No Deal* again."

"You two used to have such fun watching that together over the phone when you were out of town!"

"We did, and it was always fun debating the odds of taking the sure thing against the temptation." Charles was enthused.

"I've seen temptation," acknowledged God.

"Hey, God?"

"Yes, Charles."

"Can I tell you something that involves alcohol?"

"I think I can handle it."

"Becky's turned our place upside down and can't find my special margarita recipe. She tried to make 'em this afternoon."

"Did she get it right?"

"No, she way overdid the tequila."

"Like that's an accident!"

"Hey, God?"

"Yes, Charles."

"You remember my Aunt Ethleen? Uncle Charles died probably twenty years ago."

"Very practical lady."

"That's her. Well, she told Becky that sometimes Uncle Charles doesn't even seem real to her. That shook Becky up."

God understood. "It is a path the one left behind walks alone."

"Hey, God?"

"Yes, Charles."

"Today is probably the first day since her mama and I died that Becky did not receive a card from somebody."

"Is she hurt about that?" God was curious.

"Oh, no," Charles was quick to say. "I think she just recognizes it as a milestone, the beginning of people going away. Of course, it's inevitable."

"Well," said God, "I don't go away."

"Hey, God?"

"Yes, Charles."

"Do you think reminders are okay?"

"What do you mean, Charles?"

"Well, everywhere Becky looks, wherever she goes, whatever closet she goes into, or drawer she opens, there are reminders of me. There is no piece of paper or pencil or clothing that I touched that's insignificant to her. It seems comforting some of the time but also painful."

"Charles," God reassured, "pain is part of the process."

"I hate that for her," Charles sighed.

"Me too, Charles. Me too."

"Hey, God?"

"Yes, Charles."

"Becky keeps struggling with that whole prayer thing."

"How so?"

"Well she gets e-mails all the time like my so and so is cured because prayers were answered, and she's like, *Why weren't my prayers answered?* She just can't figure it out."

"Nobody," said God, "has it completely figured out."

"Hey, God?"

"Yes, Charles."

"Since I died Becky's been given at least two really good packages of coffee."

"And?"

"She doesn't know how to make coffee, not a clue how to set up that coffeemaker."

"Another division of labor?"

"Yep."

God grinned. "You two are cute."

"Hey, God?"

"Yes, Charles."

"You've got to watch Becky's daddy a little closer."

God chuckled. "That man is a moving target."

"I know. Becky was down there all day Friday and Saturday because he hurt himself picking up her mama's hospital bed. Finally, they went to the emergency room, and they sent him home. Then he had to go the doc, and they scheduled an MRI, but for the wrong thing, so she had to take him back. And they still don't have the results."

"Sounds like I need to be watching the health-care providers."

"Hey, God?"

"Yes, Charles."

"It's getting harder and harder for Becky to know how to respond when people ask her how she's doing."

"Tell me what she's been saying," God requested.

"Oh, the usual, staying busy, trying to take care of her dad, one day at a time—all that."

"Well, that's all true," God pointed out.

Charles wasn't ready to let it go, "Yeah, but there's so much more."

"There always will be," God warned.

"Hey, God?"

"Yes, Charles."

"Becky's getting more vocal over this prayer thing."

"Well," God reasoned, "maybe talking about it will be enlightening."

"Yeah, but she may have hurt somebody's feelings talking about how she gets e-mails that say 'Oh, my hangnail is better, so my prayers have been answered.' Pisses her off, if I may say so."

God didn't take issue. "She's pretty angry right now."

"Hey, God?"

"Yes, Charles."

"Becky talked to our family doc today. He's been really good to her."

"Glad to hear it."

"You know he told her he was cutting back on his hours, and I was part of the inspiration for that."

"Charles, you are nothing if not inspirational!"

"Hey, God?"

"Yes, Charles."

"Becky had her first formal meeting today about Bob."

"Your brother." It wasn't a question. "How'd it go?"

"She felt like she was drinking out of a fire hose, as I used to say, and well I guess I still say. Anyway, trying to figure out who's who—who all his doctors and therapists and caregivers are. Rita, our oldest daughter, went with her. Then they went to the hospital to see him. Seems like his progress is slow."

"I'm sure she recognizes that none of that support matters if he doesn't get better," said God.

"Exactly. It's like her watch now."

"Hey, God?"

"Yes, Charles."

"Folks are still calling to check on Becky."

"Sweet."

"Yes, but sometimes she feels that if she tells them the truth, they'll commit her."

"That," said God, "is why sometimes you just don't answer the phone."

"Hey, God?"

"Yes, Charles."

"Becky's in Tampa today. She flew down there with Pam for the girls' Final Four. First trip she's done for pure fun."

"Good for her," said God.

"Good for Pam," said Charles.

"Hey, God?"

"Yes, Charles."

"Becky wonders if she's different, if her pain is different."

"Is that how she sees it?"

"She doesn't want to voice that because it is arrogant, but inside she wonders."

"Charles, you two were special together. The fact that other people are special too doesn't change that."

"You know, God, it's not like we never hurt each other or didn't screw up—oh, sorry."

"Go on."

"But we did have something special."

God smiled. "I know you did, Charles."

"Hey, God?"

"Yes, Charles."

"Every day is a new insult."

"It won't always be that way."

"Why don't you tell that to Becky."

"I'm trying, Charles. I'm trying."

Hey, God? Yes, Charles.

"Hey, God?"

"Yes, Charles."

"Becky just thanked me for always changing the cat litter."

God smiled. "Sometimes it's the little things."

"Hey, God?"

"Yes, Charles."

"I don't know if there has been more discussion about medicine and miracles or if Becky is just more sensitive to it. Doesn't she need to leave the door open for miracles?"

God was kind. "It's okay, Charles. That door is shut for her right now."

"Hey, God?"

"Yes, Charles."

"Becky's working today . . ."

"On Saturday?"

"Yes, at home, trying to get year-end accounting stuff caught up, but what's cracking me up is that she's playing all her sad songs in the background on the laptop."

"You're cracking up because she's playing sad songs?"

"Well, no, not that part, but in the past she wouldn't have had a clue how to even do that."

"She can be taught," God observed.

"Hey, God?"

"Yes, Charles."

"Becky's going to miss Easter at our church since she's in Pennsylvania. But she's wondering what kind of deal that is in heaven. I've been kinda wondering that myself."

"You know, Charles, every day is Easter here."

"Hey, God?"

"Yes, Charles."

"Did you see that?"

"No. I can't be everywhere."

"Huh?"

"Just a little God joke, Charles."

"Hey, God?"

"Yes, Charles."

"Let's try this again. Did you see that?"

"What?"

"Becky was just outside walking Millie, and she looked up at the cloudy sky and said, 'Where are you?' Then over to the west was a small patch of perfect blue sky, right among the gray clouds. She said, 'Oh, there you are.'"

"Then what?" asked God.

"She just kept her eye on the heavens until she and Millie came on in."

"Hey, God?"

"Yes, Charles."

"At church today, Daly asked Becky how she was. She said she was good. She lied."

"I forgive her," God promised.

Hey, God? Yes, Charles.

"Hey, God?"

"Yes, Charles."

"Gann called Becky again tonight."

"Every Sunday night." God had noticed. "You guys have some good friends."

"Don't we know it," said Charles.

"Hey, God?"

"Yes, Charles."

"Becky's going crazy tonight. You know who's helping her?"

"Winkum?"

"Yep, our oldest cat. She's sticking right with Beck, just talking to her."

"Cat therapist."

"Hey, God?"

"Yes, Charles."

"Becky took all four animals to our vet today—doc told her Winkum probably wouldn't last the year."

"That's hard to hear."

"It really was—Winkum's a good kitty. I know they're not equal but—"

God finished the sentence. "The losses are mounting up."

"Hey, God?"

"Yes, Charles."

"Great gal from church, Mary, met Becky for dinner to-night. She told Becky her favorite memory of me was my talking about that ice fishing trip."

"You and Tom had a blast, but I didn't see all that much fishing going on." God grinned.

"Oh, you saw that?" Charles grimaced.

"I see everything."

"Uh oh."

"Hey, God?"

"Yes, Charles."

"MaKayla just told Becky, 'I wish Papa would come back.'"

"Oh, Charles."

"Hey, God?"

"Yes, Charles."

"Becky quit this morning."

"Too much?"

"Yep. Sick father, sick cat. Too much."

"She'll be back."

"Already is."

"Hey, God?"

"Yes, Charles."

"You know Beck's sweet SGIGs (you know – the Steel Got It Girls?) are plotting to give her a kitten because Winkum is sick."

"I doubt Becky needs to replace her, especially in your condo."

"For sure, plus Winkum is saying, 'Hey, I ain't dead yet.'"

"Still," smiled God, "sweet thought."

"Indeed."

"Hey, God?"

"Yes, Charles."

"Becky was afraid to skip another morning. She had to show up at the gym just to keep 'em from giving her another cat!"

"Hey, God?"

"Yes, Charles."

"Have you noticed how Becky examines different pictures?"

"Photographs of you?"

"Yes. In a way, she tries to look through to my aorta, to see if she can tell what stage it's in or when it started to be a problem."

Head shaking, God replied, "Not unreasonable in a weird way."

April 26, 2008

"Hey, God?"

"Yes, Charles."

"I died five months ago today."

"Correct."

"Becky's trying to think if, since the very first time she saw me in high school, she's ever gone five months without seeing me."

"Well, she's gotta know I see you, Charles."

"Hey, God?"

"Yes, Charles."

"Today Becky looked at my picture, and for the first time, thought I might really be dead and won't be coming back."

"That's progress."

"But God, it's been five months."

"Take it, Charles."

"Hey, God?"

"Yes, Charles."

"Becky opened my Bible tonight to read a verse at random hoping it would be a message."

God was in teacher mode, "Becky is going to have to work a whole lot harder than that."

"Hey, God?"

"Yes, Charles."

"You know I was telling you about Winkum?"

"Um hmmm."

"Becky has a real bottom line on that."

"Which is?"

"She doesn't want a new cat and she doesn't want a new husband."

"Winkum stays and you come back?"

"You got it."

"Hey, God?"

"Yes, Charles."

"We're now in the fifth month."

"Yes."

"And Becky still cries every day."

"Sometimes, it just sneaks up on her."

"Hey, God?"

"Yes, Charles."

"Becky's decided she's a bit envious of older people when they lose their spouses."

"Why?" God was curious.

"Because there's more acceptance by society that their hearts feel broken and they may very well look forward to joining their spouse soon. And it's not really all that unexpected when that happens."

"So if Becky were older . . ."

"Maybe she could have those feelings without having to hide them."

"Hey, God?"

"Yes, Charles."

"I think the devil's got Becky all tangled up in her underwear. Think she'll be all right?"

"Absolutely," God replied quickly.

"Are you sure?"

"Hey, I'm God."

"Hey, God?"

"Yes, Charles."

"These kids are killing me. MaKayla just said, 'I really wish Papa was still down here.'"

"Hey, God?"

"Yes, Charles."

"You know before I died Becky never really understood why people who lost someone concentrated on what that loved one would have wanted them to do."

"She's getting insight now."

"Well, yeah, it's like she is just clueless."

God understood. "I did see her write in her journal, *'Just tell me what to do.'*"

"Hey, God?" Charles was laughing.

"Yes, Charles."

"Maddie just asked Becky if she could play with the little handheld calculator. Becky got it out for her, and Maddie looked up and said, 'Remember when Papa said I was just a calculating *fool*?'"

"Hey, God?"

"Yes, Charles."

"Wise people tell Becky that with time this will get better."

"That's true," nodded God.

"But Becky's problem is that it is better, but so what? What she wants is for it to be the *same*."

God and Charles recognized the futility of a reply.

"Hey, God?"

"Yes, Charles."

"Oh my gosh. Did you see the book MaKayla wrote? Her third grade teacher had all the kids write and illustrate a book. It's bound, hard cover—the real deal. And . . ." Charles paused for effect, "it's dedicated to me."

God smiled. "Dedicated to *Papa*."

"Got that right," Charles beamed.

"Hey, God?"

"Yes, Charles."

"Becky gets up in the morning thinking she can't make it through the day, but every day she does."

"And every day she will." God was sure.

"Hey, God?"

"Yes, Charles."

"Becky was driving home today from Shelbyville. It was cold and cloudy, very overcast. She kept looking up at the sky, trying to see through all the layers to us in heaven."

"Did she have an idea?"

"I think so. Thought she could see us above it all with brilliant streams of color and light."

God nodded. "Pretty close."

"Hey, God?"

"Yes, Charles."

"Becky puts on my cologne. See anything wrong with that?"

"Nah," God sniffed. "Smells good."

May 17, 2008

"God?"

"Yes, Charles."

"Our thirty-ninth wedding anniversary is in twelve days."

"Wow, Charles, that is wonderful."

"Don't we know it. But she is worried about this day. Will it be a celebration or a wake?"

"She's got twelve days to decide."

Hey, God? Yes, Charles.

"Hey, God?"

"Yes, Charles."

"I feel bad when Becky has to go to bed alone. She hates that. Did you know her earliest fantasy of marriage was the idea of curling up each night with her husband? We really did do the spoon thing."

"I feel bad about that too," said God.

144

May 26, 2008

"God?"

"Yes, Charles."

"Becky's having a hard time today. It's the six-month anniversary of my death."

"Oh my."

"BJ called and Beck was crying. BJ told her tomorrow would be six months and one day."

"That's true."

"Yes. And her mother's birthday."

May 27, 2008

"Hey, God?"

"Yes, Charles."

"Today's Becky's mama's birthday."

"I know Charles. She's right here."

"Easy for me and you God, not so easy for Becky and her daddy. She did get to spend the day with him."

"I saw that. They went to the cemetery."

"She cooked him a couple of pork chops too. You know veggie girl doesn't do that for just anybody!"

May 29, 2008

"God?"

"Yes, Charles."

"Today's our thirty-ninth anniversary."

"So you said. Becky doing okay?"

"You know I think so. I think she's realizing we had more together than some folks ever get. But she is wearing my cologne again."

"Charles, that's okay."

"Hey, God?"

"Yes, Charles."

"Barnes called Becky today."

"Course he did. Thirty-nine times now."

"Every anniversary for thirty-eight years, and you know she asked him at my funeral if he was going to keep calling."

God was pleased. "I love that boy."

Hey, God? Yes, Charles.

"Hey, God?"

"Yes, Charles."

"Did you see that fire in the kitchen?"

"Charles, I did. Your wife has got to pay attention."

"God?" Charles was concerned.

"Charles, she'll be fine."

"Hey, God?"

"Yes, Charles."

"Becky is going to finish up the few things we wanted to complete in the condo."

"Is there a problem?"

"Well, like everything else, she worries she shouldn't be doing anything like that."

"Her lists are therapy. She's got to do it." God was sure.

Hey, God? Yes, Charles.

"Hey, God?"

"Yes, Charles."

"Becky figured out how to put a new bag in the shop vac yesterday."

"Never done that before. Did it make her mad?"

"Not as much. She just sat down on the floor and read the instructions over and over and over."

"Hey, God?"

"Yes, Charles."

"No offense, but could you work on this aorta business?"

"None taken." God was not insulted. "They're perfect when they leave here."

Hey, God? Yes, Charles.

Lay down beside me
Love me and hide me
And don't every wander away.
(Alison Kraus)

"God, Becky's been listening to this a lot."

"It's beautiful, Charles."

"Hey, God?"

"Yes, Charles."

"Rita called Becky tonight. On the phone sixty-seven minutes, just going over stuff."

"That kid," said God, "has stepped up."

"Odd, isn't it?" mused Charles.

"Not really," said God. "Ang will too."

Hey, God? Yes, Charles.

"Hey, God?"

"Yes, Charles."

"There's soap suds in our guest bathroom toilet."

"Huh?"

"Yeah, Becky heard gurgling and went to find the noise. Then she called Gary and told him she could wash dishes in there."

"Did he tell her what to do 'til the plumber can get there?"

"Oh yeah."

"Good ole Gary."

"Hey, God?"

"Yes, Charles."

"The plumber came early Saturday to look at the soapy toilet. Becky was reminded that something interesting always happens when I'm gone."

"Like the time she put the pasta down the garbage disposal, it quadrupled in size, and the repair cost $200?" God was laughing. "I think you were in Mississippi."

"Exactly. I was in Boston when Becky sent me a cell phone picture of the yellow tape, fire truck, and police officer in front of our house."

"That," agreed God, "was rather entertaining."

"Hey, God?"

"Yes, Charles."

"Becky wants to keep my cell phone and my voicemail but Rita needs a phone so they went to the Verizon store today."

"Were they helpful?"

"When the gal figured out what was going on, she helped Becky sort out how to rearrange the phones, manage the cost, and still keep my voice mail and messages."

"And," God was tuned in now, "Becky's figured out how to work her own Blackberry and the Bluetooth *and* the e-mail. Surprised?"

"Uh yeah," said Charles, "but not any more than she is!"

"Hey, God?"

"Yes, Charles."

"Becky is engaging in a little deception."

"Like what?"

"Like learning to tell people what they want to hear."

"Hey, God?"

"Yes, Charles."

"Ali, our neighbor, came over again last night and brought Becky pumpkin cupcakes—still warm. She doesn't think Becky is eating enough. Another neighbor invited her out next weekend."

God smiled. "Now that's what I'm talking about."

"Hey, God?"

"Yes, Charles."

"Becky is so sick of feeling sorry for herself."

"Charles," God said kindly, "it's okay. Losing you is big."

"Thanks, Boss."

"Hey, God?"

"Yes, Charles."

"You know that video they made for my service? Do you think Becky watches it too much?"

"Doesn't matter," said God. "Eventually it will be a comfort."

"Hey, God?"

"Yes, Charles."

"Becky's standing out on our terrace, asking, "Why Charles? Why not me?"

"And," said God softly, "if it had been reversed, you'd be asking the same."

"Hey, God?"

"Yes, Charles."

"Becky can't figure out how to sleep at night."

"I know, Charles."

"She tries one pillow then two, but nothing is me."

"Of course. It's still just a pillow."

"Hey, God?"

"Yes, Charles."

"Becky wants me to come home for one night. Just one night. She won't tell anybody."

"Now, Charles."

"I know."

"Hey, God?"

"Yes, Charles."

"Guess Becky's discovering the obvious."

God looked up quizzically.

"No matter how much she cries, or rants, or gets mad at You . . . when she wakes up the next morning her mama and I are still gone."

"Hey, God?"

"Yes, Charles."

"Becky asked her shrink for a script."

"You mean as in what to say to people?"

"Right—something accurate, not phony, but she can say without crying."

"And the winner is . . ."

"I'm making progress."

God approved. "That's a fair statement."

"Hey, God?"

"Yes, Charles."

"Becky has to make her own tea in the mornings."

"What about it?"

"I used to always make it for her."

God got that. "Another reason to miss you."

"I gotta be honest, God. I miss doing it."

"Hey, God?"

"Yes, Charles."

"Becky got home today, and Rita and Ali had roses and a card and a bottle of wine waiting for her."

"Nice. Nice. Nice."

"I hope they know how much I appreciate that."

"Hey, God?"

"Yes, Charles."

"Becky had a session with her shrink today—been a tough week."

"Oh, I see that—her mama's birthday, your anniversary, cousin's grandson in that horrific car accident."

"And she still struggles with how to keep me around, how not to act like I never existed."

"Now, Charles," God promised, "you are unforgettable. That won't be a problem."

"Hey, God?"

"Yes, Charles."

"A funny thing happened when I was in the ICU. Becky tried to take my picture."

"Did they let her?" God looked surprised.

"Oh no, they 'bout tackled her."

"Why'd she want a picture?"

"Well, BJ was there, and they decided when I got well and we were all partying, they wanted me to see what I looked like—all those tangles of wires. Didn't think I'd believe it!"

God was solemn. "Becky never thought you would die."

"Right."

"Hey, God?"

"Yes, Charles."

"Becky's been reading all the books that are supposed to help you deal with loss. Mostly they just make her mad. She's taking issue now with one that says bartering is one stage of grief except in death. It says, 'You don't barter when someone has died.'"

"Not true," said God.

"Exactly. I know you remember that time she was begging you to let me come home for just one night. She wouldn't tell anyone."

God nodded. "Just shows the experts don't know everything."

"Hey, God?"

"Yes, Charles."

"Becky went to Home Depot today to get a holder for the garage wall for mops and brooms and stuff."

"I love Home Depot," said God.

"Oh, for real, they've got more stuff than, well . . . You."

God chuckled. "Did she find what she wanted?"

"Yes, but then she had to ask for help to figure out what kind of anchors she'd need."

"Good," said God. "She can ask for help."

"Hey, God?"

"Yes, Charles."

"Did you hear what Keith just said? '*I miss him. Life's just not as much fun when he's not around. But I bet heaven is more fun.*'"

"Right-o, Charles!"

"Hey, God?"

"Yes, Charles."

"A funny thing just happened. Becky looked up and said, 'Charles, we're making you out to be a saint down here and a saint you ain't!'"

God grinned. "Becky's pretty smart."

"Hey!" Charles retorted, even if it was God.

"Hey, God?"

"Yes, Charles."

"Do you know my absense leaves a physical ache for Becky?"

"I created love good." God was not going to apologize.

"Hey, God?"

"Yes, Charles."

"Becky keeps trying to work out this prayer thing in her head."

"What part now?"

"Well, she doesn't really think prayers work, yet she is comforted when others pray for us."

"Well," said God, "people learn sooner or later that prayer doesn't operate like a help desk."

"Hey, God?"

"Yes, Charles."

"Becky was driving down Moore's Lane today and remembered the night we rescued that cat that had been hit. I parked in the middle of the road so nobody would hit him again, and Becky thought we were all going to end up run over. She wants me back so she can yell at me again."

God cackled. "Women!"

"Hey, God?"

"Yes, Charles."

"Becky asked her shrink today if she's going to be miserable forever. Doc said no."

"Probably doesn't believe that right now."

"Probably not."

"Hey, God?"

"Yes, Charles."

"Becky had lunch with Tracy today. She can really appreciate the loss Tracy and Robert and Taylor experienced when baby Ryan died."

God was interested. "I heard them sharing ideas about what it's all about."

"You know," said Charles, "Tracy and I used to do that a lot."

"Oh," said God. "I always got the biggest kick out of you two."

"But," Charles was going in for the kill, "I was right wasn't I?"

"Aw, Charles, everybody's right in heaven."

"Hey, God?"

"Yes, Charles."

"Whiz has been helping Becky with all the financial stuff. The first time she met with him, they talked about a lot of things—all us high school buddies and the bunch that came to my service. He told Becky the day meant so much that he didn't want to leave."

"It really was a rock-n-roll day, my friend."

Hey, God? Yes, Charles.

Hey, God? Yes, Charles.

"Hey, God?"

"Yes, Charles."

"Sometimes Becky just wants to be enlightened about the simplest things."

"Like what, Charles?"

"Like, how can somebody just be gone?"

"Hey, God?"

"Yes, Charles."

"Becky is not happy with herself. She thinks her mind is preoccupied to the detriment of other people."

"Are you talking about the grocery store parking lot?"

"Yes. She rolled through the stop signs and was too far gone before she saw the mother pushing out the cart with two kids."

"Well," conceded God, "she needs to get a grip. But they weren't really in danger."

"Hey, God?"

"Yes, Charles."

"Rita is having to take Granddaddy to the ER!"

"Oh, no."

"They can't lose him too."

"We'll do the best we can, Charles."

"Hey, God?"

"Yes, Charles."

"Becky's having coffee in the morning with Daly."

"Your pastor? Little overdue."

"Oh, he's tried, and she's been putting him off. He usually thinks outside the box, and she doesn't think he'll try to snow her with religious claptrap, but she wanted to feel a little more in control just in case."

God nodded. "Not good to deck your pastor."

"Exactly."

"Hey, God?"

"Yes, Charles."

"She didn't have to deck him."

"So good to not knock your pastor out at the bagel place."

"Not only did he not tell her my death was 'God's will,' he made a point to say he didn't believe it could be."

"Good man." God was satisfied.

"God?"

"Yes."

"Daly told Becky he felt I could see and hear and know what she's doing. It was a great relief to her to hear someone—especially our pastor—say that."

"I bet."

"She told him that when she thinks—or writes—it's a three way communication."

"Clearly."

"Hey, God?"

"Yes, Charles."

"When Becky and Daly were about done at the bagel place, Daly told her he didn't have all the answers."

"Honest," said God.

"Becky told him she would be suspicious if he did."

"She's not the only one," said God.

"Hey, God?"

"Yes, Charles."

"Becky ran into our upstairs neighbor last night. She asked Becky how she was doing—then told her she needs to eat."

"Nice neighbors over there."

"You bet—Becky went inside and cried at the kindness."

"Hey, God?"

"Yes, Charles."

"Becky just left our financial advisor's office. The practical side of death is weird, isn't it?"

"I guess it is Charles. You can raise all the hell you want but the electric bill will still arrive right on time."

"Hey, God?"

"Yes, Charles."

"You know in the hospital Becky begged me not to leave her."

"I know that."

"She even offered to take my place."

"Charles, everybody tries to bargain."

"Hey, God?"

"Yes, Charles."

"Millie just can't figure out where I am."

"I know."

"Couldn't I let her know—she's a dog—who's she gonna tell ..."

"Charles," sternly ...

"Okay, okay ..."

"Hey, God?"

"Yes, Charles."

"You know that CaringBridge site Markham set up when I was in the hospital? Did you see that sweet note from JJ?"

"Lotta' sweet notes. But didn't you hire him?"

"I did and he said when I left the company he cried—that I was like a grandfather to him."

"Grandfather?" God was howling. "Ouch."

"Hey, God?"

"Yes, Charles."

"Becky's making a pot of tortellini soup today."

"Yum."

"We used to do that together. I chopped up all the onion and garlic."

"You're a good husband, Charles."

"Hey, God?"

"Yes, Charles."

"I just love Keith. He and Pam and Becky were talking yesterday about a family member that might need some help. Keith said that's what families do."

"I love him too," said God, "and Pam."

"Hey, God?"

"Yes, Charles."

"Becky mailed two sympathy cards this week."

"That's nice."

"She just has realized how much that means to people."

"I know her mailbox has become very important to her."

"Hey, God?"

"Yes, Charles."

"Aunt Shirley was telling Becky that she was just amazed at all Becky keeps doing. Becky credited adrenalin but Aunt Shirley said You were giving her the strength."

"Becky buying it?"

"Not really. She values Aunt Shirley's opinion but thinks You wouldn't have to be giving her strength now if You'd answered her prayers in the first place."

"I," said God, "can handle the attitude."

"Hey, God?"

"Yes, Charles."

"Armstrong called Becky today."

"On a Thursday?"

"Exactly. She and Becky work together on Wednesdays but yesterday Armstrong had an appointment so Becky was not expecting to see her. When Armstrong and Kerry came by for a few minutes, I don't think Becky had her game face on. Armstrong, being Armstrong, picked up on that."

"You know Charles. It's okay for Becky to feel what she feels."

"I know, God, but Becky thinks other people shouldn't be so subjected to it."

"God?"

"Yes, Charles."

"Have you noticed that Becky's just about quit praying?"

"I have."

"Although the other day she sent up a quick one for Cheyenne almost without thinking."

"Muscle memory, Charles. I'll take it."

"Hey, God?"

"Yes, Charles."

"Becky's listening to Kathy Mattea's 'Where've You Been?'"

"Sweet song."

"You know Becky and I agreed we'd wind it up around age ninety—give or take—and go out together."

"Well," said God, "that was one plan."

"Hey, God?"

"Yes, Charles."

"Becky heard a leveling comment today."

"Which was?"

"*Life really is fair. It ultimately breaks everyone's heart.*"

"Hey, God?"

"Yes, Charles."

Charles was excited. "You will not believe—well yeah you would—Chris called Becky. The national User's Group is going to honor me at their upcoming annual meeting."

"Charles! What a true tribute to you."

"Thanks, God."

"Hey, God?"

"Yes, Charles."

"Roger and Gloria have asked Becky to come to Guatemala and work for a week."

"Well you both always wanted to go."

"I know. Becky's thrilled—wishing I'd be with her though."

"You will be, Charles."

"God?"

"Yes, Charles."

"All the 'help' materials seem backward to Becky."

"Why?"

"She says they're all about her—and she thinks it ought to be about me."

"You know that doesn't make any sense."

"She just knows I didn't want to die."

"Well", said God, "it all worked out."

Charles replied carefully, "For me and You maybe."

"Hey, God?"

"Yes, Charles."

"Ri said something the other day about her mother being 'on the market.' "

"Oh, what did Becky think about that."

"Thought it was really weird."

"Kids will sometimes start at the end."

"I don't think that's the end in Becky's mind."

"Hey, God?"

"Yes, Charles."

"Becky is so excited the User's Group is going to honor me at their annual meeting—says I'll think I'm hot stuff."

"Hot," God was practically smirking, "being a relative term up here."

"Hey, God?"

"Yes, Charles."

"Becky wants her mama."

"I know Charles. But we have her now."

"Hey, God?"

"Yes, Charles."

"The idea of death used to chill Becky, but now she welcomes it whenever it's time."

"But nobody," said God, "knows when that is."

Charles's eyes narrowed. "You don't organize that do you?"

"Don't tell anybody."

"Hey, God?"

"Yes, Charles."

"I've been thinking about our conversation yesterday."

"Knew you would."

"You could. You just choose not to."

"Well, Charles, that works on so many levels."

"Hey, God?"

"Yes, Charles."

"Becky's remembering the night we got stuck in Amarillo in the motor home. We wound up snowed in, sitting at our little table drinking wine and watching the jackrabbits run around us. Beautiful world there, God."

"Thanks, buddy."

"Hey, God?"

"Yes, Charles."

"Did you notice how the kids stepped up after I died?"

"I did," responded God.

"What a comfort. Course they all got religion at the moment," Charles mused.

"Happens all the time," said God.

Hey, God? Yes, Charles.

Hey, God? Yes, Charles.

216

*I hope you're having a good time up there
because it sucks down here.*

"God," said Charles, "did you hear Becky's comment?
Could I let her know how good a time it really is?"

"Not yet," God replied.

"God?" Charles was serious.

"Yes, Charles."

"Thanks for letting me run by the apartment and visit with Becky one more time for those few minutes after I died and she had come home from the hospital. We appreciate that."

"No problem," said God.

"You know she didn't tell a lot of people about that visit."

God nodded, "Duh."

"Hey, God?"

"Yes, Charles."

"As you well know the docs never let me regain consciousness, had all those drugs to make me sleep and the paralytics so I couldn't move and would conserve oxygen."

"Oxygen is important," nodded God.

"But," Charles continued, "just that one time when Becky was standing there, I let that single tear roll down my cheek. Then I worried she might think I was crying for me. I heard later she knew that tear was for her and our family and friends."

"Of course she knew."

"Hey, God?"

"Yes, Charles."

"Becky has got to stop listening to Vince Gill."

"I know. Some of his songs even make ME cry."

"Hey, God?"

"Yes, Charles."

"Becky has tons of HER friends to talk to—but sometimes she'd like to talk to MY friends."

"Ooh," God was sympathetic.

"You see the problem," said Charles.

"Guys," God acknowledged.

"Hey, God?"

"Yes, Charles."

"Bettye called Becky last night. She's been such a good friend—still misses Chester after fifteen years."

"You saw him yesterday, didn't you?" asked God.

"Yep, he still misses Bettye too."

"God?"

"Yes, Charles."

"Becky was listening to a song where one lover was telling another not to leave."

"What about it?"

"When we were in ICU, she was afraid to say anything out loud that might sound negative to me in case I could hear her. So she would whisper under her breath, please don't leave me."

"Hey, God?"

"Yes, Charles."

"Lots of people still praying for all my family."

"Indeed there are."

"But I worry that Becky's not praying."

"Doesn't matter right now. She's covered."

"Hey, God?"

"Yes, Charles."

"I miss my dog, too."

"I know she misses you."

"Becky was playing an old voice mail from me on the bedroom phone, didn't even think about Millie being in the room. That dog came flying around our bed toward the phone."

"Her master's voice," said God.

"Hey, God?"

"Yes, Charles."

"Ri's spending the weekend with Becky."

"Oh good."

"Yeah, they had a great opportunity to talk last night—but you know some preacher encouraged Ri to believe You caused my death."

"Oh deliver me," God was exasperated.

Hey, God? Yes, Charles.

"Hey, God?"

"Yes, Charles."

"I'm still steaming about that fool of a preacher."

God had to laugh. "You always quoted scripture when Becky called YOU fool!"

"Hey, God?"

"Yes, Charles."

"Becky feels cheated about her mama."

"The timing and all?" God knew what was coming.

"Yes, because she was in Atlanta with me for two weeks, a little crazy after that, and then Grandma died."

"Definitely cheated," acknowledged God, "and one more thing for her to be mad at Me about."

"Hey, God?"

"Yes, Charles."

"Beck's getting awfully tired of dealing—work, health, paper ... "

"I can sympathize," nodded God, "Iraq, Darfur—I get a little tired myself."

"Hey, God?"

"Yes, Charles."

"One thing Becky tried to take comfort in . . ."

"What's that Charles?"

"Docs talked about oxygen deprivation, rehab—
she knows how I would have hated being slow."

"There are," God was very sure, "some things worse
than death."

"Hey, God?"

"Yes, Charles."

"Becky keeps telling Rita that happiness is a choice."

"Good advice."

"God?" Charles was steaming.

"Yes, Charles."

"Becky—or rather, I—got a letter today from the valve company about the valve they put in my heart. Wouldn't you think if they can track the exact number of the exact valve to the exact patient, they could also know that the patient did not survive."

"You would," said God.

"Hey, God?"

"Yes, Charles."

"Really aggravates Becky that she doesn't pray like she used to."

"Well," said God evenly, "that is her choice."

"Agreed," Charles was defensive, "but still."

"Still," replied God.

"Hey, God?"

"Yes, Charles."

"When I asked you to forgive my sins, you did, right?"

"Of course, Charles. You shouldn't have to ask now."

"I know—just always good to hear it straight up."

"Hey, God?"

"Yes, Charles."

"Becky dedicated some time in church today trying to work out this prayer thing."

"I noticed that."

"I think she's down to the Lord's Prayer, the daily bread thing—and lifting up other people's names but not asking for anything."

"I know right now," said God, "she's not going to ask Me for anything."

"Hey, God?"

"Yes, Charles."

"At church today, Joe told Becky it gets easier."

"Did that help?"

"I think she can feel less shock at what happened—maybe that's what easier means."

"But?" asked God.

"But the missing me part is harder."

"You leave a big hole," said God.

"Hey, God?"

"Yes, Charles."

"Guess what?"

"Uh, you want a bigger amp?"

"Very funny. Actually the acoustics are great up here. No, wanted to tell you—Mac and Nancy have donated a tree and it's going to be planted in my memory next Sunday at church."

"I love that church," said God.

"Hey, God?"

"Yes, Charles."

"Our little church dedicated that tree to me today. It's a dogwood."

"A dogwood?" God was pleased. "Nice. Very nice."

"Hey, God?"

"Yes, Charles."

"Uh, Becky misses, you know, me."

"Really?"

"Does that surprise you?"

"Some women her age seem to stop caring."

Charles poked out that bottom lip. "Well, you know, she was married to me."

God let out a belly laugh. "Charles Cooper, what am I gonna do with you?!"

"Hey, God?"

"Yes, Charles."

"Becky's ironing her shirt today. I used to do that for her. She always said I could do a better job."

God smirked. "You fell for that Charles?"

"Every time."

"Hey, God?"

"Yes, Charles."

"Beck's been outside, sitting on the terrace, drinking a glass of wine and looking at the fountain."

"Nice."

"Yeah, but she got up and leaned over our gate and looked down the sidewalk to see if I might be walking toward her. I thought she knew I wasn't coming back."

"That," God was patient, "was this afternoon. This is tonight."

"Hey, God?"

"Yes, Charles."

"Becky feels like she's better in some ways – thinks she finally went one whole day this week without crying – but her concentration is way off."

"Like reading?"

"Right. And this morning she drove quite a ways, in bad weather, in the dark, on the interstate before she realized her lights were not on. Maybe you need to talk to her about paying attention." Charles was hopeful.

"Maybe," said God, "I just did."

"Hey, God?"

"Yes, Charles."

"Beck went to Clarksville tonight to see Josh perform in the talent show at his high school."

"Now there," said God, "is one great kid."

"Tell me about it," smiled Charles, "but he was robbed – shoulda' won tonight—God? Couldn't you have . . . ?"

"Haven't we already had this discussion."

Sigh. "I know."

"Hey, God?"

"Yes, Charles."

"You know I told you about Josh's talent show last night?"

"Yes."

"Josh dedicated his solo to me—told the audience that I told him at our family reunion last year that if he was in that talent show, I'd be there. Josh told Beck afterward he dreamed about me and doing this song a few days ago. Sure hate I missed it."

"You didn't," said God.

"Hey, God?"

"Yes, Charles."

"You know Becky and I used to buy one lottery ticket each week. She doesn't do that any more . . . thinks it's not fun without me."

"Well y'all shouldn't have been buying 'em anyway!"

"Really?" Charles was contrite.

"Just messin' with you," smiled God.

"God?"

"Yes, Charles."

"Becky thinks she was too happy with her life."

"Huh?"

"She thought she was just trying to be satisfied with whatever happened, now she thinks maybe You thought she was feeling smug."

"Oh Charles, I don't work like that."

"Hey, God?"

"Yes, Charles."

"How'd you do that Red Sea thing?"

"All in the wrists, son."

"Hey, God?"

"Yes, Charles."

"I spend all my life—school, jobs, kids, moves, finally getting it really right, especially the last ten years—then, boom, I'm gone. Why now?"

God was matter of fact. "Ask your aorta."

"Hey, God?"

"Yes, Charles."

"Becky's always loved to read—every night. Now she can't —couldn't at the hospital either."

"She can't concentrate on anything Charles. Except you."

"Oh," said Charles, "that's sorta good/bad."

"Sorta is," God agreed.

"Hey, God?"

"Yes, Charles."

"Becky's getting a pedicure today—something else she feels funny about."

"Nothing wrong with getting your toenails cut."

"Yeah, but she saw a segment on *48 Hours* the other night where a woman's husband died and she was being given a hard time because she was doing things like getting a pedicure."

"Charles . . . they think she killed her husband."

"God . . . Becky thinks she killed me."

Hey, God? Yes, Charles.

"Hey, God?"

"Yes, Charles."

"Becky's been helping her dad—threw out seven bags of trash today. We used to laugh so hard cause Grandma wouldn't let us throw ANYTHING away."

"She's right here Charles. You can gig her."

"Hey, God?"

"Yes, Charles."

"You sure have made some good people."

"I appreciate your saying that Charles."

"God?"

"Yes, Charles."

"Could you go ahead and confirm for me that it took longer than 6,000 years to create the world."

"Now Charles, if it did, Tracy's still not gonna' believe it 'til she gets here and hears it from me."

"Well true," Charles conceded, "no hurry then."

"She'll appreciate that!"

Hey, God? Yes, Charles.

"Hey, God?"

"UmHmmm."

"Becky feels weird about the life insurance."

"How so?"

"Well," Charles explained, "she wouldn't have it if I hadn't died."

God was patient with the answer. "Sorta' the point isn't it?

"God?"

"Yes, Charles."

"Becky is in one of her defining modes again."

"What is it today?" asked God.

"She's defined me as her protector. So now that I'm gone, she feels unprotected."

God was practical. "She keeps a loaded 357."

Charles hooted. "Well make my day."

"God?"

"Yes, Charles."

"Becky bought the niche for my cremains. But she's dragging her feet. My urn is still setting on our bedroom chest. Any problem with that?"

"Oh good heavens no," God was reassuring. "She can do whatever she wants. You're already here."

"Hey, God?"

"Yes, Charles."

"My dog is looking for me."

"I know," God sighed.

"It's been months. Makes me feel bad . . ."
Charles acknowledged.

"Me too," said God.

"Hey, God?"

"Yes, Charles."

"Becky doesn't want to use up anything that's hard to replace."

"What do you mean?" God asked.

"Well stuff that I used to handle, like refilling the soap dispenser under the sink or the fridge light or the light in the microwave. She doesn't want to use all that because she doesn't want them to need replacing."

God shrugged. "Gonna have to figure that stuff out sooner or later."

"Hey, God?"

"Yes, Charles."

"Millie's blackmailing Becky."

"The dog?"

"Millicent Providence Fleming Cooper. You know when we sold our house and bought the condo, when she barked, we'd say, 'There's no barking in a condominium.' She learned not to. She'd just harrumph under her breath and that was it. But now when Becky puts her in the garage at night, Millie waits just long enough for everything to get quiet and still and Becky in bed, then she starts barking. Becky doesn't have the energy to discipline her—so she just lets her in."

"Dog's not stupid," God observed.

August 7, 2008

"Hey, God?"

"Yes, Charles."

"It's Becky's birthday."

"I know."

"Oh, of course you do – that sparrow thing."

"The wagons were circled—lunches, dinner delivered, cards, calls—Vanda and Val and Tracy throwing down that slumber party, Markham drove in from Louisville and K Bell from Atlanta . . . you know lots of people will say God is good."

"And I," said God, "will say people are good."

"God?"

"Yes, Charles."

"Maddie asked Becky today if it would be a 'long time 'til you die?' Becky tried to reassure her and told her it should be a long time—that we try to be healthy."

God was concerned. "And?"

Charles was somber. "Maddie shot back, 'Papa was healthy and he died.' "

"God?"

"Yes, Charles."

"Becky is really angry today."

"She mad at Me again?"

"Not really," explained Charles, "more at the world. And doctors who say there's a chance for a miracle. After I died, she didn't buy any of that when it came to her mama. And she was right."

"The hardest thing in faith," God answered, "is when an incorrect assumption happens to result in a correct prediction."

"Hey, God?"

"Yes, Charles."

"Aren't grandchildren precious?"

"That they are son."

MaKayla just started a story about me by saying, "Here's a good memory."

"Now we're getting somewhere, Charles."

"God?"

"Yes, Charles."

"Someone asked Becky about group counseling. But she doesn't want to talk with or about other people in a group. She wants to just think about me and her mama and feel sorry for herself for awhile."

"Whatever works," said God.

"Hey, God?"

"Yes, Charles."

"Did you know that as I was headed into surgery Charlie told me he loved me."

"Whoa. Tough guy."

"Course I said it first."

"Course."

"Hey, God?"

"Yes, Charles."

"There's a little bug crawling on Becky—she keeps blowing it off and it keeps coming back. Now she's afraid it's me. Is she crazy?"

"Maybe today, Charles."

"God?"

"Yes, Charles."

"I know I'm in Heaven and I appreciate it, I do. But why do I have sad moments when I see Becky and my children and grandchildren cry?"

"Charles," God said gently. "There will be no random bad things like what happened to your aorta last November. But Heaven is a little bit like earth in that it can be what you make it. But you know what, if you are feeling empathy for your family, I'm not going to complain."

Hey, God? Yes, Charles.

"Hey, God?"

"Yes, Charles."

"Becky never let me see her cry in ICU. But once she tried very carefully to tell me to let her know about Heaven one day. How can I do that?"

"Well," God replied, "maybe you are."

"Hey, CHARLES?"

"Yes, God?"

"You haven't told me a joke in two days—what gives?"

"Been worrying about Becky—she's not got me."

"Charles, she's got Me."

"Okay, didja hear the one about. . . "

"Hey, God?"

"Yes, Charles."

"Do you get tired of all my questions now that I'm here?"

"Oh no, Charles," God said happily, "and I never got tired of your questions before you got here either."

"Hey, God?"

"Yes, Charles."

"Becky switched her rings around this morning."

"That okay with you?" God looked at Charles sharply.

"Guess so."

"Hey, God?"

"Yes, Charles."

"It worries Becky that she can't remember the exact words of our last conversation. You know they were rushing me to surgery in Atlanta and she was trying to get out of the house in Nashville."

"She," God was positive, "will remember the part that matters."

"Hey, God?"

"Yes, Charles."

"We're all going to die sometime, right?"

"Right."

"How come we can know that *and* not know that?"

"You're human, Charles."

"Hey, God?"

"Yes, Charles."

"Becky's at the beach."

"Ah, her ocean."

"Yep, she invited the whole kit and caboodle. Wound up with Rita and the girls and Aunt Shirley."

"A great crew. How's it been?"

"Aw, you know, the first night Becky got down there alone, it was harder than she expected. I think if the rest of 'em hadn't been on the way, she'd have turned around and come home."

"Well, she's been used to going to the ocean with you."

"Yes, and she's always used the ocean as therapy."

"But this time?" God was quizzical.

"It didn't change anything."

"Won't," said God.

"God?"

"Yes, Charles."

"Becky thinks she would be willing for it to be her last day if she could have *one more day* with me."

"I heard that thought."

"But then her departure has to be arranged so it doesn't hurt anyone."

"You see the problem."

"Hey, God?"

"Yes, Charles."

"Becky's made a decision."

"Which is?"

"The rest of her life can't be resolved by friends or family or church or Dr. Davis or alcohol or exercise, and not even the ocean. She can use all the resources, but she's going to have to figure it out herself."

"Hey, God?"

"Yes, Charles."

"Becky just got back into her room from Matt's wedding."

"Sweet, wasn't it?"

"Very. But she is reminded of how much she misses having someone to tell stuff to."

"Tell me about it. Sometimes I think I'll tell Jesus, but it's like talking to myself."

"Hey, God?"

"Yes, Charles."

"You know all the issues Becky's been having with prayer?"

"I do."

"The prayer thing itself, the Sunday School class, the prayer lesson book."

"She's been fighting it," agreed God. "And me."

"I know. Then yesterday Maddie and MaKayla made several crosses at church. Just as Becky was waving bye to them in the parking lot, MaK called out that she wanted to give Nane one of the crosses she'd made. Becky walked over to the car, and as MaK was thumbing through them, she said, 'I want to see which one I want to give you.' Then she pulled it out, this precious cross she had made with the word *pray* across the middle."

"Well, well, well." God tried not to grin.

"Hey, God?"

"Yes, Charles."

"Becky finally got the interment arranged for tomorrow, but it has her shaken up."

"I know."

"She hates that the pain is reopened in this way for everyone."

"And yet," said God, "she's done the best she can. And she knows you know that."

"Good," said Charles.

"Hey, God?"

"Yes, Charles."

"The interment was today."

"I saw that."

"Rita and the girls were there with Aunt Shirley and Becky's daddy."

"Saw that too."

"And Daly said my loss was one of the greatest he had ever experienced in a church family."

"Wow," said God.

"Wow." Charles was humbled.

"Hey, God?"

"Yes, Charles."

"Becky went with Wanda and our high school buddies Saturday night to hear our old band, the Us Group, back together to play. I do miss Cline and all the gang."

"I think she enjoyed the evening."

"Me too. She didn't tell anybody the interment had been this morning. I know she felt me there with her."

"And Me." God was quite certain.

"Yeah." Charles laughed, picturing the band. "God and the Us Group."

"Hey, God?"

"Yes, Charles."

"This is the second day in a row a stranger has offered to pray for Becky. What gives?"

"Prayer," explained God, "matters."

"Hey, God?"

"Yes, Charles."

"It's November."

"I'm aware of that."

"Becky's been dreading November ever since she started coming out of the fog and realized it's going to roll around again."

"I'm aware of that too."

"She's worked really hard to get ahead of it, making plans to cover the month, keeping positive things moving forward."

"By and large, Charles, she's succeeding."

Charles gave a sigh of relief. "That she is."

"And," added Charles, "November 27 will be year two, day one."

God smiled. "Thanksgiving."

"Hey, God?"

"Yes, Charles."

"You know the last time Becky and I made love was a year ago today."

"As memory serves, you were hesitant because the grandkids were there."

"Yeah, what was I thinking? But she winked and said they'd be asleep soon enough."

"And?" asked God with a little smirk.

"And they were." Charles high fived God.

"Hey, God?"

"Yes, Charles."

"She's still paying for my cell phone."

"And?"

"God, it's been a year."

"Charles, it's ten bucks. Leave her alone."

November 11, 2008

"Hey, God?"

"Yes, Charles."

"The last time Becky and I told each other, in person, goodbye and we loved each other was a year ago today."

"You were leaving to go back to Atlanta for the week."

"I was, and she watched me all the way out of the parking lot."

November 12, 2008

"Hey, God?"

"Happy Birthday, Charles."

"Becky still has my voice mail on the answering machine at home from when I called her from Atlanta a year ago and said it's my birthday!"

"Of course she does. And today she's received all sorts of calls and e-mails and cards."

"Wow," said Charles.

"They love you, buddy."

November 13, 2008

"Hey, God?"

"Yes, Charles."

"A year ago today was the last voice mail I ever left Becky on our home answering machine. I told her I'd had a little workout."

"I know, Charles. She still listens to it."

November 14, 2008

"Hey, God?"

"Yes, Charles."

"A year ago today I went to the ER."

"I know. I was with you."

"It was the last time I talked to Becky. We just thought it was nothing."

"Hey, God?"

"Yes, Charles."

"Becky spent last night with her dad and then Rita and the girls came. Today she had dinner with the bunch."

"Still staying busy, I see."

"She calls it a moving target. You know she thinks the loss feels just as keen as ever, but her reaction has been dulled in the last year."

"Time." God was wise.

"Hey, God?"

"Yes, Charles."

"Were you in Johnson's Chapel this morning?"

"Of course."

"Did you see the flowers that Becky and the girls had on the altar for me?"

"I sure did. I also heard Daly say again you were one of the most revered memories he would have. And," God continued, "after church did you hear Richard tell Becky that when Daly asked them to think of gratitude, Richard said knowing you was one of the things he was thankful for?"

Charles grinned. "That Daly and Richard are pretty smart."

God hooted.

Hey, God? Yes, Charles.

"Hey, God?"

"Yes, Charles."

"Becky was told recently that the second year is harder than the first."

God's response was quick. "Good-god-almighty."

Charles nodded. "That's what Becky said."

"Hey, God?"

"Yes, Charles."

"Becky had dinner tonight with Wanda."

God smiled. "She's a good gal."

"For real," Charles agreed. "And Wanda's like, 'Now come Wednesday, I know you're planning to be with your daughter, but if you need me before, after, whenever, you just call me. We can butt our heads into the wall if that's what you need to do.'"

"November 26," God replied. "Like I said, good gal."

"God?"

"Yes, Charles."

"This time last year Becky was sitting in the hospital and feeling two emotions: hope that I would survive and gratitude for all we had at that moment. Look at this e-mail she sent to Your people. You know what? The words are just as true today as when she wrote them."

(E-mail from the St. Joseph's critical care waiting room, sent late Wednesday night, day eight, before Thanksgiving 2007 to so many keeping an online vigil.)

You need to have a good day tomorrow. As I sit here with a quiet moment contemplating Thanksgiving, I'd like to tell you what Charles and I are thankful for:

Family you can always count on
Friends who never disappear
Fruit that shows up when you need something healthy
Cookies that show up when you don't
Phone calls that show you care – from Minnesota to Guatemala and all points in between
Emails that you can re-read
Cousins who mobilize to take care of your parents
Dog sitters
A church family that's the real deal
Goody bags and boxes that appear with magazines and fuzzy socks and neck supports and all manner of snacks
Clean laundry and diet pepsi – delivered
People who pray
People who pass the ammunition
Open ended offers for anything
Smart people who interpret medical jargon
Hearts that just show up

Thank you.

"Hey, God?"

"Yes, Charles."

"A year ago, I was dying."

"That you were, Charles."

"And today Becky's dying a little bit."

"Charles," God reassured, "she's been dying a little every day for the last year. But she'll be okay. She has made the choice to be okay."

Charles had to laugh. "When she decides to do something . . . "

"Exactly. Remember the time her mother was in the hospital and she had all of you at her mama and daddy's house cleaning and doing laundry, and she walked by the table and some laundry she had told her daddy to put up was still laying there?"

Charles was still grinning. "Yep, Angela said to Granddaddy you might as well do what she tells you, or she'll hunt you down like a dog."

"And now," said God, "that little personality trait may work in her favor."

"I hope so," Charles sighed.

"Hey, God?"

"Yes, Charles."

"Becky's thinking about writing a book. She believes you and I will inspire her."

"Oh," God was modest, "I expect we can. You know I've inspired a few books before."

November 26, 2008

"God?"

"Yes, Charles."

"I died a year ago today."

"I know son."

"Becky set the alarm this morning at 2:40 a.m. so she'd be up at my time of death. But she woke up at 1:40, and instantly realized it was 2:40 eastern time in Atlanta. Thanks for handling that so she didn't miss it."

"Most welcome."

Hey, God? Yes, Charles.

"Hey, God?"

"Yes, Charles."

"It's been a year. Now can I let Becky know how good it is up here?"

"Son," God replied with a satisfied smile, "I can assure you she has received that message."

POSTSCRIPT

November 26, 2010

On this day, three years to the day after Charles died, Madelyn and MaKayla and I are together. They are now eight and eleven. We share good memories of Papa. At one child's suggestion, the three of us say our blessing before breakfast. The other then looks at me and says, "I know you pray for all of us each night, too."

Yes ma'am, I think. *I do now*.

ACKNOWLEDGMENTS

Hey, God? Yes, Charles. would not have found its way to a publisher's desk had not Becky Sullivan asked to share it with a friend who was hurting.

It would not have been published without the Turner Publishing team's unwavering belief that the book could help others who are hurting.

It would not have been written without the friendships of Bettye Morris, who inspired the journal, and Dr. Barbara Fleming, who suggested a book. It was our older daughter, Rita Cooper, who suggested THIS book. It meant a lot to hear the heartfelt response from our other daughter, Angela Cooper, after she first read it.

And, to all our family and friends . . . this book is in many ways a tribute to your presence—then, before then, and now. I used real names because I want you to know who you are. If for some reason your name did not get said, or you came into my life after this was written, you still know who you are.

I am grateful beyond words to each of you.

ABOUT THE AUTHOR

REBECCA COOPER is a Belmont University graduate and former teacher, business owner, and career professional. Her love of writing dates back to elementary school, producing stories, poetry, high school and college newspaper articles, and travel blogs (before she knew she was blogging.) In this first published work, scribbles on scraps of paper capture imaginary conversations she began to overhear after the sudden death of her husband. With a priority for her grandchildren, and a love for travel and books, she divides the rest of her time among church, other family, and friends—all of whom took turns carrying her along a journey of love, loss, and recovery. Becky currently resides in Franklin, Tennessee.

photo courtesy of Jan Baker

CPSIA information can be obtained at www.ICGtesting.com
Printed in the USA
LVOW11*1426091115

461711LV00014B/114/P

9 781681 620954